CITIZEN
ILLEGAL

About the BreakBeat Poets series

The BreakBeat Poets series, curated by Kevin Coval and Nate Marshall, is committed to work that brings the aesthetic of hip-hop practice to the page. These books are a cipher for the fresh, with an eye always to the next. We strive to center and showcase some of the most exciting voices in literature, art, and culture.

BreakBeat Poets series titles include:

The BreakBeat Poets: New American Poetry in the Age of Hip-Hop, edited by Kevin Coval, Quraysh Ali Lansana, and Nate Marshall

This Is Modern Art: A Play, Idris Goodwin and Kevin Coval

The BreakBeat Poets Vol. 2: Black Girl Magic, edited by Mahogany L. Browne, Jamila Woods, and Idrissa Simmonds

Human Highlight, Idris Goodwin and Kevin Coval

On My Way to Liberation, H. Melt

Black Queer Hoe, Britteney Black Rose Kapri

Citizen Illegal, José Olivarez

Graphite, Patricia Frazier

The BreakBeat Poets Vol. 3: Halal if You Hear Me, edited by Fatimah Asghar and Safia Elhillo

There are Trans People Here, H. Melt

Commando, E'mon Lauren

poems

José Olivarez

Haymarket Books
Chicago, Illinois

© 2018 José Olivarez

Published in 2018 by
Haymarket Books
P.O. Box 180165
Chicago, IL 60618
773-583-7884
www.haymarketbooks.org
info@haymarketbooks.org

ISBN: 978-1-60846-954-3

Trade distribution:
In the US, Consortium Book Sales and Distribution, www.cbsd.com
In Canada, Publishers Group Canada, www.pgcbooks.ca
In the UK, Turnaround Publisher Services, www.turnaround-uk.com
All other countries, Ingram Publisher Services International,
IPS_Intlsales@ingramcontent.com

This book was published with the generous support
of Lannan Foundation and Wallace Action Fund.

Special discounts are available for bulk purchases by organizations
and institutions.

Cover artwork by Sentrock.
Cover design by Brett Neiman.

Printed in Canada by union labor.

Library of Congress Cataloging-in-Publication data is available.

10 9 8 7 6 5

For Pedro, Ruben, & Danny

Not bad, huh, for some immigrants

—JAY-Z

Contents

I

(Citizen) (Illegal)

Mexican woman (illegal) and Mexican man (illegal)
have a Mexican (illegal)-American (citizen).
is the baby more Mexican or American?
place the baby in the arms of the mother (illegal).
if the mother holds the baby (citizen)
too long, does the baby become illegal?

the baby is a boy (citizen). he goes to school (citizen).
his classmates are American (citizen). he is outcast (illegal).
his "hellos" are in the wrong language (illegal).
he takes the hyphen separating loneliness (Mexican)
from friendship (American) and jabs it at the culprit (illegal).
himself (illegal). his own traitorous tongue (illegal).
his name (illegal). his mom (illegal). his dad (illegal).

take a Mexican woman (illegal) and a Mexican man (illegal).
if they have a baby and the baby looks white enough to pass (citizen).
if the baby grows up singing Selena songs to his reflection (illegal).
if the baby hides from el cucuy and la migra (illegal).
if the baby (illegal) (citizen) grows up to speak broken Spanish (illegal)
and perfect English (citizen). if the boy's nickname is Güerito (citizen).
if the boy attends college (citizen). if the boy only dates women (illegal)
of color (illegal). if the boy (illegal)
uses phrases like "women of color" (citizen).
if the boy (illegal) (citizen) writes (illegal) poems (illegal).

if the boy (citizen) (illegal) grows up (illegal) and can only write (illegal)
this story in English (citizen), does that make him more
American (citizen) or Mexican (illegal)?

My Parents Fold Like Luggage

my parents fold like luggage
into the trunk of a Toyota Tercel.
stars glitter against a black sky.
from the sky, the Tercel is a small lady

bug traveling north. from the sky,
borders do not exist. the Tercel stops
in front of a man in green. stars glitter
like broken glass. the night so heavy

it chokes. in the trunk, it is starless.
my parents protect this moment. this now.
what folds them into the trunk of a Tercel.
the belief that the folding will end.

it doesn't. dollars fold into bills. my parents
near breaking. broke. they protect what might
unfold them to discover they are six:
a family. if the man in green opens the trunk,

the road folds back. this moment & everything
that follows disappears into the ink of a police report.
why doesn't he open the trunk? my parents say
god blessed us. maybe they are right,

but i think about that night & wonder where
god was—a million miles away in the stars,
in the shared breath between my parents, maybe
everywhere. maybe nowhere. from the sky,

the man in green is so small it is impossible
to see him wave. from the sky, it is impossible
to hear whether my parents cheer or pray
as the car steals north.

Mexican Heaven

all of the Mexicans sneak into heaven.
St. Peter has their names on the list,
but the Mexicans haven't trusted a list
since Ronald Reagan was president.

River Oaks Mall

it's hard to hold onto a secret
whether or not anyone is looking.
when the girl i have a crush on asks

why i keep looking at her, i say it's not
like i like you, gosh. denial is
one of the best ways to confess.

when the teacher asks who brought beans
for lunch, i blame it on the boy next to me.
i bite my tongue when my stomach protests.

trying too hard is another way to confess.
my family takes a Saturday stroll
through the mall dressed in church clothes.

every other kid in jeans, t-shirts, & Jordans.
fun fact: when you have to try to blend in
you can never blend in. my dad gives me a penny

to throw into a fountain that makes dreams
come true. all my dreams except one.
my family trying so hard to be American

it was transparent.

My Therapist Says Make Friends with Your Monsters

we are gathered in truth,
because my therapist said
it was time to stop running,

& i pay my therapist too much
to be wrong, so i am here.
my monsters look almost human

in the sterile office light.
my monsters say they want
to be friends. i remember

when we first met, me & my
monsters. i remember the moment
i planted each one. each time

i tried to shed a piece of myself,
it grew into a monster. take this one
with the collar of belly fat

the monster called Chubby, Husky,
Gordito. i climbed out of that skin
as fast as i could, only to see some spirit

give it legs. i ran & it never stopped
chasing me. each new humiliation
coming to life & following after me.

after me, a long procession of sad
monsters. each monster hungry
to drag me back, to return me

to the dirt i came from. ashes
to ashes, fat boy to fat.
my monsters crowd around me,

my therapist says i can't
make the monsters disappear
no matter how much i pay her.

all she can do is bring them
into the room, so i can get
to know them, so i can learn

their names, so i can see
clearly their toothless mouths,
their empty hands, their pleading eyes.

Boy & The Belt

the belt is an extension of dad & dad is an extension of god. the boy is an extension of dad, too. the belt is just one thread tying them together. the boy prays the belt stays wrapped around dad's waist. the belt does not believe in god, but if the belt did believe in anything, the belt would call it purpose. the belt began as skin on a cow. its purpose was to protect & it failed. the boy knows all about that. the boy has purpose too. dad & god & mostly he fails. the belt's new purpose is to hold—to contain dad's expanding waist— except when the boy fights, then the belt is born again as a classroom ruler with the day's lesson. maybe the belt & the boy can rebel. the boy tugs at the thread that will bring dad & the belt. the boy won't lie about his bruised brother or call it anything noble. the boy fights because he is bigger. dad says he has no choice. the belt says it has no choice. the boy understands he displeases god. when the belt meets the boy, the belt kisses the boy & leaves purple lipstick. dad understands this as an act of love. the belt doesn't know about love. the belt knows it completed its job. & the boy hears love.

The Voice in My Head Speaks English Now

snow finds me underneath layers. maybe
the cold wants to hang out. take me skiing.
wants me to see winter isn't a bad country
& it's not, but i'm still shivering. i make snow
angels & come out snot-nosed. throat blistering.

it never stops being cold. my new voice fit
with coughing. my friends say summer is coming.
they're lying. on gray days, i wear the sun, but
it falls off my shoulders. if you catch my mom
in good light, it's impossible to tell where the sun ends.

i tell myself that's where i'm from, but i'm not
sure. when i was a baby i used to get fevers.
maybe that's why my parents planted me in snow.
now i'm a long way from the fire my parents feared
& so close to this new blue flame.

Rumors

you know how rumors get born out of spit & breath, but got whole legs
by the time they land, so that's how holding hands becomes hooking up
or pregnant. listen to everything. don't believe anything. once My Homie
Since Second Grade told me The Girl From First Period With The Cute
    Smile
was wearing a scarf to cover up some hickies & The Girl From First Period
wasn't even wearing a scarf that day. what's the difference between a lie
& a truth. a lie hasn't happened yet. we grew up on the good love songs
as well as The Juke Jams. Back That Ass Up was on the first CD I ever
    bought.
so few of us had even seen Love. we had only met Love's fucked-up cousins:
Divorce & Shouldn't You Be Wearing Your Wedding Ring. My Homie Who
Started Smoking Cigarettes In The Eighth Grade had both her parents &
    she said
they only loved each other on the 1st & 15th. my parents hadn't kissed
since the steel mill closed. that's a lie that feels true. some of us practiced
saying i love you to the mirror. that was a lie we wanted to believe.

II

Mexican Heaven

St. Peter is a Mexican named Pedro,
but he's not a saint. Pedro waits at the gate
with a shot of tequila to welcome
all the Mexicans to heaven,
but he gets drunk
& forgets about the list.
all the Mexicans walk into heaven,
even our no-good cousins who only
go to church for baptisms & funerals.

Ode to Cheese Fries

golden goo of artificial delicious,
what probably lines
my stomach with sunlike grease for weeks after
eating the yellow
so yellow it could only be manufactured. so what
if it's fake?

as much cheese content as Apple Jolly Ranchers—
i come from
a city of foreclosure foreclosure empty lot. city
where we got
dollar-store-brand action figures—so what
my Wolverine didn't

have retractable claws or the right uniform?
so my joy
at Pano's my favorite fried-everything spot—
the cashier's voice
a box of Newports filtered through throat—
i didn't know

i would miss this home where the patties
come from freezers
and maybe not ever from cows or even animals—
i live in
a city that brags about its organic fair-trade
quinoa-fed beef—

of course i miss the '90s pop playing in the restaurant—
the Backstreet Boys
live in Cal City where the band never breaks up,
the song plays
on repeat as the cashier takes my order, say it with me—
cheese fries please—

give me everything artificial including cardboard fries,
the bread fresh
out of some Walmart cloning experiment—throw in
a cold pop—
i want a joy so fake it stains my insides &
never fades away

I Wake in a Field of Wolves with the Moon

i wake in a field of wolves with the moon
howling & smack my lips.
i know no love without teeth
& have the scars to remember.

trace those scars & you have a map
to my heart. open carefully. i will not die.
i know i have teeth of my own.
there are stories about men who leave

a trail of corn husks & growing bellies
i know my reflection when i see it.
i wake among the wolves
licking dirt from their paws & know

who i am when the wolves don't attack me.
when they call me hermano & want to dap
me up. send me a full moon.
all the princesses get their crowns

burped up. you can't find love
in those stories. let my love be a wolf.
i'll lay my head on a bed of her teeth.
i know my love knows when to bite.

Note: Rose that Grows from Concrete

the inspirational slogan wants you to believe you are a rose, but consider the emperor's muddy boot. you could be a rose or concrete. the record suggests the boot sees both as a welcome mat. we need a new metaphor. a seed is better. but when seeds grow, who gets the fruit? fuck it. be a rusty nail. make the emperor howl.

Ode to Cal City Basement Parties

lights off & even
your closest homies
unfamiliar. under
ground. under
the influence.

lovers tag walls
the deep blue
of Levis. hands on
hips. hips on hips. red
Solo cups. smoke hides.
touch reveals.

there are no news cameras
& your parents off
at impolite bars, so
no one watches while you
take the light glittering
off the disco ball
& paint yourselves
brand new & shining.

Not-Love Is a Season

not-love is a season.
i drank fire. a dozen blankets

couldn't keep me from shivering.
winter is an unavoidable fact.

unless you're from Cali &
i don't trust people who don't know

the freeze of loneliness. the dead
branches abandoned

by the birds still chasing summer.
my homies all telling me

i'll meet someone else. like i want
to meet someone else. my wound deep.

but mine. already time working to ease
my grip on my hurt. i know misery

thaws. the frozen branches a blank canvas
for a brush of green. the flowers brilliant

& there like they never left. like I said,
i don't trust people unfamiliar

with love. how it begins before the sun
whispers a hot word. when the only light

received is artificial & polite as a light bulb.
how love is a season that begins like a leaf.

when in the dead winter a tree dreams
of a crown it will one day wear.

Mexican Heaven

all the Mexican women refuse to cook or clean
or raise the kids or pay bills or make the bed or
drive your bum ass to work or do anything except
watch their novelas, so heaven is gross. the rats
are fat as roosters & the men die of starvation.

On My Mom's 50th Birthday

my mom puts on makeup & she is not my mom,
not a mom at all, she is admiring how good
the red lipstick looks on her lips, she is in the ugly
bathroom with the rusty faucet that spits

cold water in the cold country she adopted,
& for what—tonight the what ifs melt
with the snow & it is not winter,
tonight, my mom is not my mom,

nor does she know any children,
tonight kids cry on someone else's bed, she is not
married, tonight her mom still nags her
about finding a man, husband

is a stain on a collar, tonight i watch my little brothers
& make dinner for my dad, i am removing my mom
from our house—god willing,
we will not destroy it—i am removing

my mom & placing her in a club in Guadalajara
with her sisters & sisters are as close to love
as she wants to be right now, dance the only work,
i am unbraiding our DNA, unknotting our lives,

so for the next few hours she will not worry
about me & my brothers, so for the next few hours
all she will have to worry about is the color of her lips
and the handsome men admiring them.

Hecky Naw

you can take the boy
but the hecky naw stays
announcing his nation
of origin shame i was
ashamed the first time
i left home i kept you
under my throat
your song a basement
juke party i was born
south side juking language
i thought i left that party
dreamt myself in an
Armani suit in an
Armani room with many
Armani suits
isn't that what Harvard
was supposed to buy
where the border ended
in a boardroom my parents
proud for once
i thought i was gone
& might come back
on some save-the-hood type shit
but the hood isn't
a garment you can toss off
it's a skin hecky naw
my classmates
giving me the look
they give lab rats
before they hit the switch
that shocks them
hecky naw
if my professors say
one more thing about

Chicago i might heck
-le them or throw eggs
hecky naw i never
could scrape myself white
hecky naw
you the music i bumped
in the night
in my headphones
when i wanted
to hear my one true name

Ode to Scottie Pippen

Scottie swatting Charles Smith
into his concrete gym shoes,
i loved you best of all the Bulls.

i was short & chubby & jumped
like i carried baby elephants
in the pockets of my gym shorts.

Scottie jumping over New York
skyscrapers, serving Mars a bucket
of shove it, a courtside seat

to watch his team bend the knee.
underneath my heart, i carry
a moldy factory manufacturing sky.

Scottie, you made it look easy,
the way your legs ate air,
found every escalator up.

i was watching your game.
working my own factory
trying to build my way out.

Mexican Heaven

Saint Peter lets Mexicans into heaven
but only to work in the kitchens.
a Mexican dishwasher polishes the crystal,
smells the meals, & hears the music.
they dream of another heaven,
one they might be allowed in
if they work hard enough.

The Day My Little Brother Gets Accepted into Grad School

he posts on Facebook, the digital block.
all his old friends & crushes come by to dap
him up. imagine the flowers they place
on his lap. he smells them, but not for long.

back when he graduated from college, he threw
his cap into the sky & it fluttered like a bird
with a broken wing. when it landed, my brother
was still broke & unemployed. the day my brother

gets into grad school, he can't afford a happy meal
& still the praise comes through: my mom thanks
god. my dad offers my brother a cold beer, which
is how my family celebrates everything: a toast.

a drink. my dad prays between gulps. my mom
drinks when god blinks. my family: two fists
colliding. nothing strong enough to stop
my parents from raising a home in a city

being razed or to stop my dad's steel mill from closing or
the foreclosure notice from landing at our doorstep,
& here we are, my brother is going to grad school:
another promise, the familiar fluttering. my brother

grown in the backwash of a cold beer. in the aftermath
of a long prayer. amongst the weeds in the vacant
lot that used to house our dreams. mixed up with dirt.
ordinary ground. no magic but water

I Tried to Be a Good Mexican Son

i even went to college. but i studied African American studies which is not
The Law or The Medicine or The Business. my mom still loved me.
so i invented her sadness & asked her to hold it like a bouquet of fake flowers.
she laughed through it all. i didn't understand. wasn't immigration a burden?
what about the life you left, i ask my mom. she planted flowers
only house on the block with flowers. foreclosure came like a cold wind.
it took her flowers. but that was a season. new house, bigger garden.
mijo, go get some tomates from the yard, is something my mom really says.
i tried to be a good Mexican son. went to a good college & learned depression
isn't just for white people. i tried to be a good Mexican son, but not that hard.
sometimes, my mom's texts get dusty before i answer. even worse, i never share
the Jesus Christ memes she sends me on Facebook. if there is a hell,
i'm going express. i hope they have wifi. i hope i remember to share
my mom's Jesus Christ memes. maybe god believes in second chances.
but i doubt it. i tried to be a good Mexican son. i came home for the holidays
still a disappointment. no million-dollar job or grandkids.
Spanish deteriorating. English getting more vulgar.
i tried to be a good Mexican son, but i kept fucking
it up. my mom still loved me. even when i couldn't understand her blessings.
she makes me kiss her on the cheek before i leave the house. she tells me
to quiet down when she's watching her novelas. she asks me if i'm okay.
she tells me i'm getting so skinny & i need to eat more frijoles. she has
the pot ready. i try to be a good Mexican son, but all i know how to do
is sit down for a good second & leave before a bad one.

I Walk into Every Room & Yell Where The Mexicans At

i know we exist because of what we make. my dad works at a steel mill. he worked at a steel mill my whole life. at the party, the liberal white woman tells me she voted for hillary & wishes bernie won the nomination. i stare in the mirror if i get too lonely. thirsty to see myself i once walked into the lake until i almost drowned. the white woman at the party who might be liberal but might have voted for trump smiles when she tells me how lucky i am. how many automotive components do you think my dad has made. you might drive a car that goes and stops because of something my dad makes. when i watch the news i hear my name, but never see my face. every other commercial is for taco bell. all my people fold into a $2 crunchwrap supreme. the white woman means lucky to be here and not México. my dad sings Por Tu Maldito Amor & i'm sure he sings to America. y yo caí en tu trampa ilusionado. the white woman at the party who may or may not have voted for trump tells me she doesn't meet too many Mexicans in this part of New York City. my mouth makes an oh, but i don't make a sound. a waiter pushes his brown self through the kitchen door carrying hors d'oeuvres. a song escapes. Selena sings pero ay como me duele & the good white woman waits for me to thank her.

Mexican American Obituary

after Pedro Pietri

Juan, Lupe, Lorena became American this way,
serving crackers at a picnic while a strange wind
swung through the branches carrying names.
Juan, Lupe, Lorena died this way, too, silently
while trump won the presidency & the police
kept killing their Black neighbors & relatives.
Juan died saying it was none of his business.
Lupe died believing their degrees would save them.
Lorena died after loading the gun & handing it over
to the policeman who aimed it at her whole family.
Juan, Lupe, Lorena all died yesterday today
& will die again tomorrow
asking Black people to die more quietly,
asking white people not to turn the gun on us.

White Folks Is Crazy

on the way to dinner,
a white boy runs past
wearing a t-shirt
& shorts as long
as my boxers.

his breath freezes
in the air & leaves
a path of clouds
in his wake.

"i don't understand
how white boys
can wear shorts
in the winter,"
i say to Emiliano.

"i know. i wear
pajamas under my jeans
& i'm still hella freezing,"
he says through gloved
hands. "you know
they gotta feel it,
shit, i feel it
just looking at them."

we step inside & wait
for the blood to slowly
repopulate our faces.

Emiliano turns back
to the ghost of the white boy,
& says, "on second thought,
white folks on TV

kill people every day
& they don't seem
to feel a thing."

Mexican Heaven

there are white people in heaven, too.
they build condos across the street
& ask the Mexicans to speak English.
i'm just kidding.
there are no white people in heaven.

I Ask Jesus How I Got So White

depending on the population of the room in question,
i get asked what i am. my mom told me i'm Mexican,
but because Mexican women can't be trusted,
some people want to know if i'm really Mexican.
because i know i'm a questionable narrator
when it comes to my own life, i ask Jesus
how i got so white & Jesus says
man,
i've been trying to figure out the same damn thing myself.

Poem in Which I Become Wolverine
after Tim Seibles

i wake up to powdered faces on the news
disagreeing politely while the ice caps melt
& bombs punctuate every day like a period.

what does peace look like but merciless war?
there are more ways to put lead in a body
than pulling a trigger.   what do you think

a food desert is   but a long sip of poison?
& you think it's spilled juice,   an accident,
as if history books aren't written by guns.

every day my people confined to a news ticker
below waving flags & rising stock prices—
eight detained in an ICE raid of El Paso—   i know

when you look at our abuelitas you see knives
in their braids,   knives in their hips,
i know you hear invasion orders when our children sing

sana sana colita de rana. just last week
two ICE officers with cuffs ready to bite
the hands of a fourth-grader.   & still

the daily calls to speak English properly,
to trade mangonadas for what type of life exactly?
what is assimilation but living death?

my enemies aren't ugly-faced crooks, they don't laugh
while innocent die.   they point & say how
tragic   then go home to pet their cute dogs.

some days when the news   is the news,
& i'm required to show up on time & polite,
i can see it like a movie. i mean   i can feel

my claws coming in,   six presidents
talking liberation,   casting votes
through steel & blood.   i mean six reasons

to end the chitchat.   i can see myself on a poster
movie or America's most wanted, posing with the head
of state.   i know what happens to Wolverine.

i know my rage is a poison.   i know it kills me first.
& still i love it & feed it.   i mean i can see it like
the last scene of a movie: good cop in civilian clothes

walking to their cop car.   my six abolitionists
counting up the score,   one against history.
i wish i could tell you   the cop gets their morning donut,

i wish i could,   roll credits.

When the Bill Collector Calls & I Do Not Have the Heart to Answer

i unbury the boy, pull him out
of the cardboard box in my gut
where i keep him gone. almost
ready for jobs like this.

the boy picks up the phone. hello,
he says. the boy wears a cracked
turtle shell. his name is my name,
but we are not the same person.

when the phone rings, & it is not
a job offer. when the voice is legal,
polite as a razor, i bring the boy.

hello, he says. yes, i am Jose Olivarez.
i play video games while the boy bites
his fingernails & listens. i look at him:
the shell on his back broke beyond repair

& too small anyway. is it loyalty that keeps us
from tossing what's not useful? the boy says yes,
& i think about napping. is loyalty another word
for fear? maybe i should grab the phone

from the boy. i am the adult, after all.
the boy starts to cry. i imagine the bill collector
lost, trying to comfort the boy who sounds like a man

because he speaks with my bass, the boy
who will inherit my bad credit, & all the mistakes
i am too small to face. it is the boy, in the end
who calculates all the lemonade stands he owes,

who promises the bill collector
he will take responsibility, who hangs up the phone
& crawls back into his shell, back inside my body,
while i stare at a blank television screen.

Mexican American Disambiguation

after Idris Goodwin

my parents are Mexican who are not
to be confused with Mexican Americans
or Chicanos. i am a Chicano from Chicago
which means i am a Mexican American
with a fancy college degree & a few tattoos.
my parents are Mexican who are not
to be confused with Mexicans still living
in México. those Mexicans call themselves
mexicanos. white folks at parties call them
pobrecitos. American colleges call them
international students & diverse. my mom
was white in México & my dad was mestizo
& after they crossed the border they became
diverse. & minorities. & ethnic. & exotic.
but my parents call themselves mexicanos,
who, again, should not be confused for mexicanos
living in México. those mexicanos might call
my family gringos, which is the word my family calls
white folks & white folks call my parents interracial.
colleges say put them on a brochure.
my parents say que significa esa palabra.
i point out that all the men in my family
marry lighter-skinned women. that's the Chicano
in me. which means it's the fancy college degrees
in me, which is also diverse of me. everything in me
is diverse even when i eat American foods
like hamburgers, which, to clarify, are American
when a white person eats them & diverse
when my family eats them. so much of America
can be understood like this. my parents were
undocumented when they came to this country
& by undocumented, i mean sin papeles, &
by sin papeles, i mean royally fucked, which

should not be confused with the American Dream
though the two are cousins. colleges are not
looking for undocumented diversity. my dad
became a citizen which should not be confused
with keys to the house. we were safe from
deportation, which should not be confused
with walking the plank. though they're cousins.
i call that sociology, but that's just the Chicano
in me, who should not be confused with the diversity
in me or the mexicano in me who is constantly fighting
with the upwardly mobile in me who is good friends
with the Mexican American in me, who the colleges love,
but only on brochures, who the government calls
NON-WHITE, HISPANIC or WHITE, HISPANIC, who
my parents call mijo even when i don't come home so much.

Mexican Heaven

tamales. tacos. tostadas. tortas.
pozole. sopes. huaraches. menudo.
horchata. jamaica. limonada. agua.

You Get Fat When You're in Love

you got a little extra love
on your ankles, love hanging
over your belt line. love makes it hard
to fit inside your pants sometimes.
love got you buying bigger sizes,
need deeper pockets for all this love.
your buttons can't hold all the love
rippling up the middle of your ribcage—
love turns those shirts into accordions.
you make music with this love,
carry yourself like a song.

    when you get skinny,
    everyone rushes to compliment you.
    they want to know what your secret is.
    tell me, they say, what's your secret?
    you look great.

        call it the Broke Heart Diet.
        love left you.
        then you left you.
        now all you have
        is this disappearing body.

Interview

after Safia Elhillo

where is your home?

in my parents' new house
there is a room for everyone
except me.

where is your home?

i went to México & no one recognized me.

where is your home?

i went to México & everyone was my cousin.
the radio played José José straight from
my mom's mixtapes. where you from, my cousins ask,
& i point at the radio.

where is your home?

it took me three years to hang art
in my Bronx apartment. soon after,
i started getting tattoos. there, i said,
i'm all moved in now.

where is your home?

riding down Lake Shore Drive
listening to GCI.
all the songs i was given
slap through the car
like the lake slaps the shore.

where is your home?

it took me three days to take down my art
& move out of the Bronx. is leaving
always easier than arriving?

where is your home?

the house i grew up in was foreclosed.
there is a small note taped to the door.
i still have the key, but the key opens nothing.

My Family Never Finished Migrating We Just Stopped

we invented cactus. to survive the winters
we created steel. at my dad's mill
i saw a man dressed like a Martian
walk straight into fire. the flames
licked his skin, but like a pet, it never bit him.
in the desert, they find our baseball caps,
our empty water bottles, but never our bodies.
even the best ICE agents can't track us
through the storms, but i have a theory.
some of our cousins don't care about LA or Chicago;
they build a sanctuary underneath the sand,
under the skin we shed, so we can wear
the desert like a cobija, under the bones
of our loved ones, bones worn thin
as thorns to terrorize blue agents,
bones worn thin as guitar strings,
so when the wind blows
we can follow the music home.

If Anything Is Missing, Then It's Nothing Big
Enough to Remember

you are born where you are born, south side, Chicago & you are born
where your parents were born, Cañadas de Obregon, México
& when you are born, your parents kiss in Chicago, & in Cañadas
your grandparents kiss. you are here & here. wrapped in blankets here,
a name shared over coffee here, you are born both places, celebration cigars
here & here, only it's hard for one body to contain two countries,
the countries go to war & it's hard to remember you are loved by both
sides or any sides, mostly you belong to the river that divides your countries,
the way a bottle drifts to shore & no one knows how far it's traveled
or where it came from, which is a lie you tell yourself, that you were not born,
you walked out of Lake Michigan, something to explain your half-everything,
all-nothing nature, it's a lie, & you know it's a lie because your
grandparents visit & the first time you meet them, they know
your name & have pictures of you, & when they return to México
your cheeks are still wet from kisses, you know your picture
is walking around the same town your parents grew up in,
you are here & here. & it is beautiful sometimes like on birthdays
when the whole yard is full of dancing & the kitchen is hot
with tortillas y tacos, here you are safe & whole & there is no
Rio Grande splitting you, mostly you scissor yourself along the lines,
you choose a side, you cut & cut & one day you wake up
& the voice in your head speaks English, you stop coming around here,
the old photos fade down here, your name mispronounced
here on your own tongue, your grandparents graying like
your memory of them & you graduate from college, & your
classmates say you must be so happy to be so American now,
& your other classmates say you must be so happy
to leave behind Calumet City & you don't know what you left
because you had been trying to leave so much, it's hard to tell
what you lost, what you kept, & what the price really was.

Sleep Apnea

i wake up with last night/ spilling into my morning/ wake up with owls/ flicking their lashes/ at me/ wake up/ but don't/ wake up/ dragging/ all my dreams/ by the ear/ like misbehaving children/ my unruly hunch/ i'm trying to tell you/ the night is never done with me/ by 1 pm the moon tries/ to escape my mouth/ stars glitter my tongue/ coffee is how i keep daylight burning/ a lemon wedge/ of night sky/ under each eye/ colleagues compliment/ the grind/ the show no tell/ i tug the evening/ behind me/ like a black velvet cape/ thick enough to swim in/ to sleep under/ velvet threatens/ to swaddle me/ swallow me/ when i sleep/ i don't sleep/ the doctor says obstructed airway/ & i hear/ what i already knew/ i got a big mouth/ i got bigger dreams/ i have a medical condition/ the doctor tells me/ sleep apnea/ & i say yes/ i am the son of immigrants/ but what does that/ have to do with sleep

Mexican Heaven

Jesus has a tattoo of La Virgen De Guadalupe
covering his back. turns out he's your cousin
Jesús from the block. turns out he gets reincarnated
every day & no one on earth cares all that much.

Note: Vaporub

vaporub is pronounced vah-po-ROO. like loud or CHEW. the label for vaporub says it's for cough suppression, but in my house, vaporub is for headaches, sore muscles, nightmares, & everything else. put some vaporub on my dad's diabetic toes & watch the sugar evaporate. miss a day of church? put some vaporub on your forehead & watch forgiveness flush your cheeks. put some vaporub on our bank account and watch the bill collectors stop calling. when i forget a word in Spanish? take a teaspoon of vaporub under the tongue.

Summer Love

like,   when you are making coffee,   you look up & see
a rifle at your head.   just a split second.   just enough
      to get your heart rate up. you don't tell anyone
about these visions.   too much History Channel as a kid.

well, things with the girl go smooth except every time she leaves,   you're
            convinced she will   never contact   you   again that she will
      disappear   into   Facebook.   you see camouflage helmets
in pizza shops.   heat-seeking missiles in the bathroom

      reconnaissance planes in your refrigerator.   an endless supply
of guns at   your   chest.   what does it mean.   your girl
      kisses you on   the neck.   you read Lucille Clifton in bed.
      do i need to say it? you are smitten   way past a little bit.

you get a new job. more money. more power. you see soldiers. more guns.
      what does it mean. you don't have a problem.   you're fine.
      the girl dumps you   at the train station. she kisses
you on the mouth,   then boards the train   to get the hell away.

            after she leaves,   you hope   the next train will unload
      an entire militia.   the visions stop.
            just like that.   you are healed.
                  or some bullshit.

V

Mexican Heaven

it turns out god is one of those religious Mexicans
who doesn't drink or smoke weed, so all the Mexicans
in heaven party in the basement while god reads
the bible & thumbs a rosary. god threatens to kick
all the Mexicans out of heaven si no paran
con las pendejadas, so the Mexicans drink more
discreetly. they smoke outside where god won't
smell the weed. god pretends the Mexicans are reformed.
hallelujah. this cycle repeats once a month. amen.

Poem to Take the Belt Out of My Dad's Hands

in this story, he is wearing the belt instead of bringing it down. my ass stays soft. my head hard. in this story, the belt hangs in his closet. i snatch it & bury it. in this story, the belt acts alone. it is not his hands. he is watching TV. SportsCenter or whatever. he would stop the belt if he could. in this story, i grab the belt & beat myself with it—in this story, it is my own hands. his hands stay innocent. i stand above myself and it is for my own good. in this story, i bury the leather belt in a cement coffin. i eat a whole cow and wear the skin like a luxurious silk. in this story, i am waiting for the whip. in this story, i am already crying. in this story, he doesn't reach for the belt. the belt is buried. he reaches for my head and rubs it. soft. he says it's okay. in this story, there is no but. this story ends here. my dad. me. still under his hands. still crying.

My Mom Texts Me for the Millionth Time

the phone vibrates/ my mom buzzes my desk/ her love reaches me/ wherever i am/ which is usually/ unavailable/ my mom home with my family/ minus me/ might as well/ be my name/ it's our family's second house/ in Calumet City/ after the first was lost/ to anachronisms/ you can find my mom/ on the couch/ her shoes off/ her bare feet/ throb with her American ache/ her work will wake her/ in a few hours/ to frame a store/ my mom's work is turning sanitary/ into pristine/ but you already know/ my mom's work/ by its invisibility/ my mom shopping with you/ watching you spill mountain dew/ on her floors/ my job takes me away/ from home/ so i can build a bridge back/ to the living room/ where my mom rests/ her feet/ awash in the glow/ she makes/ so effortless/ it's impossible/ to tell the light/ comes from her own body

I Loved the World So I Married It

music, even on the day my grandma died
there were mangos though i tasted nothing.

but slowly i came back to the world & carne asada.
better than i remembered, smoke off the meat. i could not

contain my happiness even though it felt offensive
to smile with my grandma buried & getting eaten

by the flowers. & sometimes, i look at my love &
think i would like to stay, to put a welcome mat

on our doorstep with our names hyphenated.
when i was young i believed in forever. then

my uncle died & i knew forever included none
of my family, included no friends, their stories

rotting in my head until i lose them again, so
i know i will divorce the world & let it keep

my most treasured possessions: a six-piece
with lemon pepper & mild sauce on, all the honey

of a slow kiss, my Apple Music playlists,
the way mi abuelita smiled & called me Lupito.

i hated that name except when she said it.

Love Poem Feat. Kanye West

on our first date
you arrived fashionably—
after my second beer—
just as the waiter was about
to offer me the Stood Up Special.

when you tell the story
you say it was Kanye.

how i swooned
the second you mentioned
College Dropout & it's true
my love language is the sped-up
soul sample on Slow Jamz.

i don't know how love works
but i remember the day

my grandma died
we talked on the phone.
i don't remember what you said
or whether it helped.
i only remember
when i called you answered.

for Erika

Getting Ready to Say I Love You to My Dad, It Rains

i love you dad, i say to the cat.
i love you dad, i say to the sky.
i love you dad, i say to the mirror.

it rains, & my mom's plants
open their mouths. my dad stays
on the couch. maybe the couch opened

its mouth & started eating my dad.
i love you dad, i say to the couch,
its tongue working my dad like a puppet.

i hear the rain fall & think the city is drinking.
or making itself clean. i am here
with my dad & the TV & the TV drones

on & on, so i'm not sure i hear it—
my dad grunting and nodding,
not the mushy stuff i was expecting,

neither of us cry, no hug or kiss.
a grunt & a nod. i love* you dad,
i say to my dad. we sit together

and watch TV. outside it rains. my dad
turns the volume up. the city is drunk.
the city is singing badly in the shower.

---

* America loves me most when i strum a Spanish song. mi boca guitarrón. when i say
me estoy muriendo, they say that's my jam.

i killed a plant once because i gave
it too much water. lord, i worry
that love is violence. my dad is silent

& our relationship is not new or clean.
i killed a plant once because i didn't give
it enough water. my dad and i watch TV

on a rainy day. we rinse our mouths
with this water.

River Oaks Mall (Reprise)

we were so American it was transparent.
Southpole hoodie & a i-could-give-a-fuck type
attitude. french fries down our throats.
blood pressure bursting. thin, fair
white women in our fantasies. in our faces,
our grandmothers' faces. so what?
we pawn it at the mall for a gold star.
a stamp of approval across our stomachs.
2Pac's less militant children.
it's not that we don't want to be Mexican.
we love tacos, we reply.
where does that voice come from & why
does it sound so white? later, we run back
to the pawn shop to ask for a refund,
but México is hip now. the pawn shop
is a shrine to Selena. they charge Mexicans
triple to get in. it's not that we hate
where we're from. it's just
we spent so much on name-brand clothes
& even if the fit chokes the neck,
the name still looks good
emblazoned in gold, doesn't it?

Gentefication

i plant a grain of sand in the new-organic-juice spot
en el barrio. soon, donkeys shit big stinky shits
on carrot containers. our tíos y tías smoking cigarettes
& taking up all the plugs. the grain of sand grows
into a cactus & mi Abuelita Jacinta is back
with the living. she's kicking the juicers out
of her kitchen & making masa. the whole block
heard what's happening, & outside the hydrants
open and flood the streets. the bad news is
the property value is going down again.
the bad news is white people are taking kale
with them. the good news is my boy Nate
is teaching poetry workshops in the shade.
Gwendolyn Brooks smelled the tamales
& came down to write. rejoice in the good news.
my dad comes through with a cooler
of beer & no one gets drunk enough to fight.
my mom's french braid gets longer every minute.
soon it will be long enough to toss to our cousins
in México. in LA. in Texas. there are Mexicans in DC
who got the call. Salvadorans bringing pupusas.
from the cactus, we get a steel mill.
from the steel mill, we get more tortillas.
the bad news is the economists say there is zero
economic value on our block. the good news is
we threw away the economics textbooks.
we trade tortillas for haircuts, nopales for healthcare,
poems for groceries, & if all you can do
is eat the food, we ask that you wash your dishes.
the donkeys bless everything we grow.
from the tortillas, we get more desert,
& from the desert, we get low riders. cars bounce.
our cousins in gangs get their bendiciones
from our abuelitas. the whole block is alive

& not for sale. the treaty of guadalupe hidalgo rescinded.
it's happening on our block & maybe it's happening
on your block. the bad news is the president
sends the national reserve. the good news is
they'll never find us. we pack everything
into the trunk of a Toyota Corolla. when la migra comes,
their dogs bark & spit, but all they find is grains of sand.

Guapo

i start with my feet because i hardly ever look
at them to say hello. hello, left foot. hello, right foot.
i give my feet my favorite name.
the name my mom gives me when she brags
to relatives. *Que Guapos*, i say to my best kick.
my awkward dance partners. my friends in almost
catching the beat. i move up through the hairy
terrain named my legs. *Guapo*, i say to moonlight
skin. *Heartbreaker*, i say to my thighs, ass, and dick.
my lover took all her pet names when she left.
my name doesn't belong to her now. *Ay Papi*, I say
to the scar on my belly. i only knew my name
when it came out of her mouth. *Aye, Shawty, What It Is*,
i say to my freckled chest. to the red bumps i used
to hide under t-shirts. ugly as all hell, but all mine.
my chest so pale it glows in the dark. *Guapo*
i say to the lanterns i carry. my red beard.
i give myself all of the names i like. *Young Josélito*,
Papi Churro, Lupe. shout out my hair while
i still have it. shout out my hairline & how
it makes me look like my dad. my face i got from
my mom. we look the same when we are laughing.
Guapo, i say. it is my new name. it is my old name.
it is my only name.

Acknowledgments

shout out to the editors of the following publications for publishing poems from this collection, sometimes in different forms: *Cosmonauts Avenue*, *Hyperallergic*, Mass Poetry's "Poem of the Moment," *Poets House*, the Academy of American Poets' "Poem-A-Day," the *Adroit Journal*, the *Chicago Dispatch*, the *Rumpus*, the *Shallow Ends*, *Vinyl Poetry & Prose*, & *Yemassee Journal*.

i learned how to write at Young Chicago Authors' Louder Than A Bomb Poetry Festival & at Wordplay Open Mics. thank you to my first teachers, Mr. Mooney, Michael Haeflinger, Kevin Coval, Sharrieff Muhammad, Idris Goodwin, Anna West, Avery R. Young, Felicia Chavez, Tara Betts, & all of the staff members, Wordplay features, & peers who passed through YCA. thank you to my mentors at Harvard University, Glenda Carpio & Eric LeMay.

shout out & gratitude to the people who read early drafts of this manuscript & helped turn it into a real-life book: Nate Marshall (mi hermano), Pedro Olivarez (my brother), Eloisa Amezcua, Jasmine Sha-Ree Sanders, Ben Alfaro, Araba Appiagyei-Smith, Ydalmi Noriega, & Kevin Coval.

gratitude to Sentrock for creating the perfect cover art for this book.

shout out the universe for blessing me with the most genius & loving & foolish set of friends i could ever ask for. thank you Nate Marshall, Araba Appiagyei-Smith, Lamar Appiagyei-Smith, Ben Alfaro, Diamond Sharp, Jasmine Sha-Ree Sanders, Britteney Black Rose Kapri, Eve Ewing, Christian Starling, MC Curley, Lisandra Bernadet, Morgan Parker, Adam Levin, Jamesa Marshall, Emiliano Bourgois-Chacon, Carlos Andrés Gómez. my Conversation Literary Festival family: Cortney Lamar Charleston, Hanif Abdurraqib, Angel Nafis, Paul Tran, Danez Smith, Nabila Lovelace, Jeremy Michael Clark, Safia Elhillo, Desiree Bailey, A. H. Jerriod Avant, Elizabeth Acevedo, Sean Mega DesVignes, Ishmael Islam, & Jayson P. Smith. shout out my Poets House fam: Noel Quiñones, Zakia Henderson-Brown, Emily Brandt, Chialun Chang, Alex Cuff, Rico Frederick, Anne Lai, Cynthia Manick, Nicole Shanté, Lauren Clark, & Adam Fitzgerald. shout out more beloveds: Kaveh Akbar, Fatimah Asghar, Jamila Woods, Jovanny Varela, Ydalmi Noriega, Kaina Castillo, Suzi F. Garcia, Mahogany L. Browne, Patricia Smith, Aracelis Girmay, Willie Perdomo, Aja Monet, Ada Limón, Ron Villanueva, Jon Sands, Aziza Barnes, Julian Randall, Joy Priest, Oscar Sandoval, Ryan Smith, Adam Sellers, Don Swibes, Raych Jackson, Dimress Dunnigan, Fatimah Warner, Maura Mathieu, Elysa Severinghaus, Lucerito Ortiz, Dometi Pongo, Dianna Harris, Daniel Kay Hertz, RJ Eldridge, Blue Bellinger, DJ Ca$h Era, Daniel Martinez, Memo Duarte, Sofía Snow, Stephany Cuevas, Joseph Rios, Kima Jones, Franny Choi, Lauren Jackson, Madison Smith, Sam Sax, Mark Cugini, Hieu Minh Nguyen, Miles Hodges, Naiomy Guerrero, Peggy Robles Alvarado, Andrea Flores, Jacob Saenz, Paula Ramirez, Karla Reyes, Langston Kerman, Adam Falkner, Lauren Whitehead, Renée Watson, Ellen Hagan, David Flores, Ama Codjoe, Marcus Wicker, William Camargo, Shaun Peace, Ben Spacapan, Kimanh Truong, Camonghne Felix, Weslie Turner, Adan Figueroa, TF North Classes of 2005–2008, River Oaks Mall, Halsted Street, PBHA, the Bronx, Mexicans everywhere, mild sauce, the 2010–11 Chicago Bulls, rap music, Vince Staples, A Tribe Called Quest, Scottie Pippen, Michael Jordan, Dennis Rodman, & my therapist.

thank you to the Adirondack Center for Writing, Art Institute of Chicago, Bronx Council on the Arts, National Museum of Mexican Art, Lincoln Center Education, Mass Poetry, Poetry Society of America, Poets House, Poetry Foundation, Conversation Literary Festival, Urban Word NYC, & Young Chicago Authors for supporting my work as a writer & teacher.

i wrote large sections of this book while in close conversation with students. thank you to everyone who has ever taken a workshop with me. in particular, this book was written in conversation with Victoria Chávez Peralta, Luis Carranza, & Ken Muñoz.

thank you to Julie Fain, Jim Plank, & the whole team at Haymarket Books for supporting my vision & being partners in the work.

gratitude and love to Erika Stallings & our wolves.

thank you to my mom & dad, Maria Olivarez & Pedro Olivarez, for making me so handsome. & you know, for everything in my life. i hope i make you proud. i love you.

this book is for my brothers, Pedro Olivarez, Ruben Olivarez, & Daniel Olivarez—the funniest people i've ever met. you teach me how to laugh. you teach me how to grow. i'm proud of you. thank you for leading the way.

& for you, dear reader, this book is for you.

About Haymarket Books

Haymarket Books is a radical, independent, nonprofit book publisher based in Chicago. Our mission is to publish books that contribute to struggles for social and economic justice. We strive to make our books a vibrant and organic part of social movements and the education and development of a critical, engaged, international left.

We take inspiration and courage from our namesakes, the Haymarket martyrs, who gave their lives fighting for a better world. Their 1886 struggle for the eight-hour day—which gave us May Day, the international workers' holiday—reminds workers around the world that ordinary people can organize and struggle for their own liberation. These struggles continue today across the globe—struggles against oppression, exploitation, poverty, and war.

Since our founding in 2001, Haymarket Books has published more than five hundred titles. Radically independent, we seek to drive a wedge into the risk-averse world of corporate book publishing. Our authors include Noam Chomsky, Arundhati Roy, Rebecca Solnit, Angela Y. Davis, Howard Zinn, Amy Goodman, Wallace Shawn, Mike Davis, Winona LaDuke, Ilan Pappé, Richard Wolff, Dave Zirin, Keeanga-Yamahtta Taylor, Nick Turse, Dahr Jamail, David Barsamian, Elizabeth Laird, Amira Hass, Mark Steel, Avi Lewis, Naomi Klein, and Neil Davidson. We are also the trade publishers of the acclaimed Historical Materialism Book Series and of Dispatch Books.

Also Available from Haymarket Books

No One Is Illegal: Fighting Racism and State Violence at the U.S.–Mexico Border, Justin Akers Chacón and Mike Davis

Radicals in the Barrio: Magonistas, Socialists, Wobblies, and Communists in the Mexican-American Working Class
Justin Akers Chacón

The Mexican Revolution: A Short History 1910-1920
Stuart Easterling

My Mother Was a Freedom Fighter
Aja Monet